The Survivors

Recovery Through Grief Support Groups

by

Joan Harmon

DORRANCE
PUBLISHING CO
EST. 1920
PITTSBURGH, PENNSYLVANIA 15238

The contents of this work, including, but not limited to, the accuracy of events, people, and places depicted; opinions expressed; permission to use previously published materials included; and any advice given or actions advocated are solely the responsibility of the author, who assumes all liability for said work and indemnifies the publisher against any claims stemming from publication of the work.

Dorrance Publishing Co
585 Alpha Drive
Suite 103
Pittsburgh, PA 15238
Visit our website at *www.dorrancebookstore.com*

ISBN: 978-1-4809-4102-1
eISBN: 978-1-4809-4125-0

Thanks for this book being in print goes to:
God
Jim Moore—for, production, layout and design
April Strauch—for her editing
R. Kenneth Heim—for checking my scripture choices
Katherine Fisher—who wrote the preface
Phyllis Michael—who encouraged me to continue to write
Dotty Moore—writer and friend
Many others—who encouraged me over the years to continue
working with the bereaved
Survivors—everywhere

PREFACE

In 1980, Joan (Whitmire) Harmon was a single mother with a successful career as a psychiatric nurse at Danville State Hospital, Danville, Pennsylvania.

One summer day, Lonnie, her 26-year-old daughter, struck a match to light a gas water heater. It exploded causing extreme burns to Lonnie. Lonnie died 6 1/2 weeks later.

Joan's faith in a loving God was given a difficult test. Would Joan and her faith survive? She began seeking and finding; and seeking and *not* finding answers to that question. It was a painful process.

After her recovery, people sought her help. She began developing and holding grief workshops throughout the area. One of these workshops spawned "Survivors," a support group which has become the model for others.

Because of the need for—and interest in—grief support groups, Joan has decided to share what she has learned in her years of research and experience.

Joan *has* survived and healed. She wants others to realize that there *is* life after death for those who seek it.

Kay Fisher

CONTENTS

THE REASON I DO WHAT I DO NOW:
2 Cor. 1:3-4
"Praise be to the God and Father of our Lord Jesus Christ, the Father of compassion and the God of all comfort, who comforts us in all our troubles, so that we can comfort those in any trouble with the comfort we ourselves have received from God."

The Ryrie Study Bible, New International Version.

On a beautiful summer day in 1980, I was happily enjoying my daughters and my grandchildren when my life changed abruptly. My beautiful 26-year-old daughter, Lonnie, struck a match to light a gas water heater. The heater exploded, causing burns over 75% of her body. She died 6 1/2 weeks later. Saying I was devastated is an understatement.

I will share with you some things I learned in my search for healing. I pray that, through my loss and recovery, you might find comfort for your pain or gain insight in helping others get through tragedies in their own lives.

Once upon a time…
That is how a story starts.

BUT THIS IS NOT A STORY
This is real life
real pain
real tragedy
and how we cope.

This is about feeling…
Feeling we cannot go on
Feeling we can never function again
Never love again
Never laugh again.

Is the earth still revolving?
Why are there cars on the streets?
Children going to school?
People going to work?
They are laughing.
How can they laugh?

Why are they acting like nothing has happened,
going on as if life is still the same?
Life will never be the same.
LIFE WILL NEVER BE THE SAME!

THE VACUUM

People have varied ideas on the subject of grieving. A griever will say that grief is more than to be sorrowful, more than to be distressed. It manifests itself in sickening waves of agony. The mix of thoughts, fears, and feelings is overwhelming. Something is missing—someone is missing, not coming back.

Life in our eyes doesn't seem fair. After working for years, a couple looks forward to retirement. With a mate gone the survivor faces a life of loneliness instead of spending the "Golden Years" together. A young couple's baby, longed for and loved, dies soon after birth. A beautiful teenager about to start college with a promising future ahead is killed by a drunk driver. The list goes on. So does the pain for the survivors.

Emotions go up and down. As we grieve we put on a false front. If someone approaches with a, "How are you?", we respond with a simple, "Fine", even though we are anything but fine on the inside. Friends, neighbors, co-workers, even family members expect instant recovery from grief, especially if this is a first experience with death of a loved one. The healing does not come quickly or easily. Rather, it is a long process of walking one step at a time, one day at a time through a long maze seeking comfort.

Who can help take away the pain? Jesus can. He tells us in scripture that He can lift our burdens and walk with us through our trials. He hears and answers prayer. Sometimes when grieving we want another person to talk with us and listen to us. Jesus also tells us to care for widows and orphans. What a ministry this can be. Jesus can help. We can help too. Many people need the comfort and assistance of others to return to a productive lifestyle. Churches have an opportunity to minister to this need through grief support groups.

Group support is not for everyone. If a good support system exists with friends and families, some grievers may not attend. On the other hand, others will tell you they feel like they are going crazy.

One gentlemen sat on my porch and cried uncontrollably for a long time after his wife died. He was seeing a psychiatrist, a psychologist and taking medication but not getting any better. After he started attending a weekly men's group, he began to heal. He is once again singing in the church choir, teaching a Sunday school class, and working at a part-time job, even though retired.

A woman whose husband died at age 50, after battling a heart condition for four years, was in her own words, "a basket case, nonfunctioning, cried all the time." She attended a women's weekly group and now, two years later, she is working as a professional with retarded clients. She also helps others by giving her testimony in church groups or grief groups. Both of these people credit group meetings for their recovery, as do other healing group members.

We can put our lives back together after the death of a loved one. Life will never be the same, but it can be good, although different.

Do not waste your grief. After the pain eases, find a helpful ministry to ease the pain of another. Fill the vacuum with something worthwhile.

WHO NEEDS GRIEF SUPPORT

My daughter was 26 years old when she struck a match to light a gas water heater. It exploded, and burned over 75% of her body. She lived 6 1/2 painful, difficult weeks before she died.

After her death and my search for healing, I became aware that some thoughts and feelings were not new. The pain, anger, depression, not caring whether or not I got out of bed, had been real to me in the past. My experience with a painful divorce many years before my daughter's accident had produced similar symptoms in my life as I worked through that difficult episode.

In divorce, like death, the family is cut apart. One person is no longer there. I grieved for the death of my marriage and would later grieve for the death of my child. I smiled as I worked in a hospital as a registered nurse and took care of my patients, but inside I was in pain. It was difficult handling life's daily problems alone.

As we look at others going through divorce, we need to keep in mind that in some ways it is different from death. Yet in many ways, the thoughts, feelings, and emotional ups and downs are the same. We grieve!

Although my child was 26 years old when she died, a mother who loses a young child to death will hurt just as much as I did. Accidents happen to small children and the family is just as devastated. We grieve!

A child that is carried in the body of a loving, caring mother for nine months, only to be stillborn, causes pain. Planning for a new baby, preparing a room, having high expectations that crumble, leave arms that are empty, and dreams gone. We grieve!

If a child is less than perfect, mentally and/or physically, parents can expect to have feelings of grief. "Why did this happen to my baby?" The tears, the anger, the depression, as we adjust to the news of our child's condition are normal responses. We grieve!

If a fire takes all our earthly possessions, we ask the same question: "Why did this happen to us?" We cannot believe everything is gone. We can never replace the things we love, things we saved for many years. There are pictures of our families that no one else had, special items made for us personally by someone who cared. We grieve!

A patient is told by the family physician that due to an accident, disease, or injury, part of the body needs to be removed. The same questions, thoughts and feelings will be present. He grieves!

Our only child runs away. Our lives have revolved around this child, but for some unknown reason, his or her desire for seeing the world is stronger than our close family ties. Our hopes and dreams are dashed and we are alone. We grieve!

She thought she could not manage a pregnancy. People told her it was not a baby, just a piece of tissue. Her friends and family wonder how this could have happened to such a nice person. A quick trip to a clinic and it is gone. She grieves!

They put every cent they had into a business venture, and borrowed more, absolutely sure this would support their families. Though they worked day and night and did everything they could, it failed. They grieve!

The list goes on.

The pain goes on.

We all grieve.

GUIDELINES FOR STARTING GRIEF SUPPORT GROUPS

Make people aware of the group being formed. Suggestions for informing are as follows:

1. Church bulletin on Sunday morning
2. Monthly church newsletter
3. Local newspaper article
4. Personal invitation
5. Local ministerium

Set time and place for the planning meeting.
1. Invite key members of the congregation who could be interested.
2. Mail a personal newsletter to each and ask for reply regarding attendance.
3. Invite honorary advisors who have experience working with grieving people and may be willing to share their expertise with others. Some suggestions follow:
   A. Members of clergy
   B. Local morticians
   C. Nurses

Organize at initial meeting:

1. Decide how often to meet, where and when.

    A. Large group sessions are more productive for grievers to regain social skills, get out of the house and learn how to function without a loved one. This group may meet once or twice a month.

    B. Small group sessions are more fruitful for normal thoughts, fears, feelings that grievers can share and discuss while seeking mutual answers. This group may meet weekly in the evening. You may want to start both groups according to the needs of your area.

2. Choose officers: a director, secretary, publicity person, treasurer, someone to make coffee, etc.

3. Seek leaders of meetings who are warm, caring, friendly people.

4. Plan details for monthly, or bimonthly, meetings including potential speakers and topics for discussion. Plan to vary the meetings into several different types, such as: educational, just for fun (perhaps a picnic setting in the summer), superficial (such as coping skills) and deep discussions with thoughts and feelings.

5. Pinpoint specific needs for the group such as the following: those who have little, or no, family support in the area, some having difficulty re-adjusting to aloneness after a loved one's death and those who have been unable to return to church or social functions. There will be no shortage of examples in your area.

HELPFUL LOCAL AGENCIES:
1. Area Agency on Aging
2. Home health and visiting nurses groups
3. Local morticians
4. Senior citizens groups
5. Churches
6. Hospice

SURVIVORS GROUP
LARGE GROUP SETTING

A large group is normally more than twelve people. Chairs all face the same direction. A podium may be used, if desired.

If a speaker is used for the meeting, the group could begin as follows:

SURVIVORS

A. Greetings—"I would like to welcome you all to our Survivors' Support Group Meeting today… We are so glad you are here."

B. Introductions—"As you know, I am_____(name), your group leader for today."

C. Identification—"As you came in, there were name tags for you to put your name on so that we all know who you are. I see you have them in place. If you were missed, we want to be sure you get one."

D. Prayer—"Let's start with a word of Prayer. Lord, help us to be aware of the needs of those around us and be better equipped to help each other as we progress through the hard work of grieving. We need your support and encouragement. Help us support and encourage each other, Amen."

E. Speaker—Introduce speaker. Have speakers keep message short, about 20 minutes. Grieving people do not always want to concentrate for long periods, depending on how long it's been since the death of the loved one. Try to have speakers who have experienced the death of a loved one or someone from a professional group who deals with grieving families regularly (such as nurses, doctors, funeral directors, pastors, social workers, representatives from the Area on Aging, home health and hospice teams, etc.).

F. Thank speaker for message.

G. Discussion—Refer to discussion questions under small group sessions. Discuss topics that are instigated by attendees according to their concerns. Leader may encourage interaction with leading questions, such as, "Have others in the group experienced similar situations?"

H. Praise people for willingness to seek help in a group setting. Remind them of the importance of returning to social settings even though isolating oneself at home is easier, following the death of a loved one. (This step helps individuals heal quicker and better as they meet together and discuss concerns.)

I. Read minutes from last group meeting and discuss.

J. Set time and place for the next meeting.

K. Have light snack if it is the desire of the group to do so—coffee and cookies, iced tea and donuts, etc. may be served at small tables, thus encouraging interaction of members.

L. Adjourn the meeting.

SURVIVORS GROUP
SMALL GROUP SESSIONS

A. Environment:
   1. If group is less than 12, place chairs around a table or in a circle. Some people prefer the table setting especially if books, booklets and pamphlets are used. Some may bring a tablet to make notations, to review at home, or to record names and phone numbers of group members to call at a later time.

B. Introduction:
   1. Name tags may be used or people can each introduce themselves aloud.
   2. Leader starts first by saying, "My name is_____ and yours is _____?"

C. Prayer:
   1. Leader may start by asking God to help each person as problems are discussed and to help each with the healing process.

D. Discussion—led by leader.
   1. Questions used to start or to keep group interaction going can be:

A. What problems did you have this week that you would like to discuss with the group?
   1. Has anyone else had that problem?
   2. What did you do about it?
   3. How did it make you feel?
   4. How else could it have been handled?
   5. Did anyone help you or did you handle it alone?
B. Topics listed in this book may be used or members may have their own concerns to share with the group.
E. Group may be dismissed as the group chooses, or by the leader after interactions are completed.

GUIDELINES FOR GROUP LEADERS

1. Pray for your meetings and grieving group members. Pray that you, as leader, will do a good job with these hurting people.
2. Make all group members welcome and help them feel at ease during meetings.
3. If no one starts discussion, be prepared to use a topic from this book.
4. If people in the group do not talk, try occasionally directing a question to them, such as, "Have you ever had that problem?" You may only get a "No", but you may also get people included in conversation who had previously not been participating.
5. Praise accomplishments, no matter how small. A little bit of progress to one person, may be a real milestone to another.
6. Be positive. People need to know there is improvement ahead because, often times, they do not see it initially.
7. Make meetings pleasant, laugh. Do not approach others with a glum expression. Some grievers feel they will never laugh again. They are surprised to discover meetings are not going to be depressing, boring and dreary.
8. When someone begins to cry, as they will when discussing their pain, make group members aware that crying in the group is acceptable. Ask a crying member if he or she wants to continue

talking or wait until later to continue. Wait for person to gain composure if they chose to continue.

9. Encourage members to report on each week's activities and to include the good, bad and difficult. It will help others in the group as they see people with similar problems making progress.

10. Do not rush the group. Members may need to meditate on a question or statement that has arisen. Allow this quiet time. It can be productive.

11. It is good if members of a group are in different stages of grieving. The newly grieving can have hope they will improve, as they see the healing that has taken place in another.

12. Do not reject members from attending group as long as they feel they need it. As they totally heal, they will drop out themselves.

13. Make members aware that progress is sometimes slow. Encourage them not to get discouraged with setbacks.

14. Be a good listener and encourage group members to do the same even when the same story is told repetitiously. People need to repeat things out loud as they progress through healing.

15. Keep good books available for the group to borrow and return at the meetings. Morticians, Christian bookstores and pastors may have books or booklets for educational purposes.

16. Encourage members to invite other grievers to the group. Helping each other through the grieving process is essential.

17. If the group becomes too large, you may decide to split into two smaller groups and meet two different evenings per week.

18. Remind members frequently that grief is a normal response to the pain of losing someone very close. The feelings the griever is experiencing are okay to express. They will pass as the griever works through the grief.

19. Dismiss the group when the group is ready. Do not watch the clock to dismiss in exactly one hour. Members may need to talk longer. Be prepared to allow whatever time is needed.

ACTIVITIES FOR GRIEF GROUPS

The following are suggestions of things group members can do to increase effectiveness and stimulate interest and involvement:

1. When someone in the community has a death in the family, stop for a visit. Tell the person about the group and invite him or her to attend, when they are ready. Call again later and offer to escort person or provide transportation as needed. This is especially helpful for the first meeting.

2. Start a "Buddy" program. Let each member know the names and phone numbers of those people willing to talk anytime, regardless of the hour.

3. Invite each other to meet for lunch, a walk, or movie in between meetings—especially those having the most difficulty.

4. Plan short bus trips together to areas of interest.

5. If distressed people miss meetings, telephone or visit to encourage a return to the group. Again, drive them to sessions if needed.

6. Start a Survivors library. Lay out books and booklets you have read and discuss the value of each. As funds are available, you may want to buy a book a month for book lending. Churches may make small donations to groups if they know about the library.

7. Tell people about the group so they can refer others in need.

8. Design your own flyers for advertisement. Keep churches and morticians supplied. Carry one in your purse or car to hand out as needed.

9. Make holidays special. For some grievers, group members may be the only support they have. Make favors for snack time, small gifts at Christmas, birthday cards etc. Be creative.

TO OUR READERS

This section is designed to help you as you begin a support group at church, senior citizen center, hospital or wherever you see the need. Your plans have been made. Now you ask, "What can we talk about to get our meetings started?"

The following, is information that pertains to grieving people. Information is arranged in small segments so it can be read and discussed at your regular group meetings.

There are questions at the end of each topic that you may use, or you may think of some others more appropriate for your group. You will also find recommended scripture verses. You may use these or choose your own to discuss.

May God bless your new group and may it grow steadily. I pray that many people, through attending and participating, will progress to a complete recovery from the pain of acute grieving.

Again, this reminder: If the group has topics of their own they want to discuss do not feel you must use one from this book each session. Be flexible. Talk about whatever is on the hearts of the people. Use these when there is a lull or when a topic is needed to start meaningful discussions.

You will find a large margin on each page to provide space for your personal notes or journaling. Writing your thoughts and feelings will be helpful to you as you recover or aid others in their recovery.

TOPICS TO DISCUSS DURING GRIEF SUPPORT GROUP MEETINGS

1. The shock
2. Why did this happen?
3. Anger
4. Crying
5. Unrealistic expectations
6. The guilt
7. Depression
8. Loneliness
9. Physical and emotional symptoms
10. Making only little decisions
11. Physical health
12. Intensity and duration of grief
13. Drugs and alcohol
14. Making bargains with God
15. Listening as therapy
16. Words that hurt
17. Ways to help
18. Anticipatory and preparatory grief
19. Those special days
20. Other major losses

OH! THE SHOCK!

If someone knocks on your door in the middle of the night and tells you that your 21-year-old son in college, the one you are so proud of, has just been killed in an automobile accident, your first response will probably be shock.

"OH, NO!"

Your mind races, "Things like this don't happen in my family. This is something you see on television, hear on the radio, read in the newspaper. Death isn't something that happens to me. Murders, suicides, tragedies of any kind, will not happen to me, only to other people."

After working with over 200 terminally ill patients, Elizabeth Kubler Ross, wrote the book "On Death and Dying" in which she discusses basic stages that she found happening in the lives of those facing death. She lists five stages many people experience. Some people say there are as many as ten stages or, as few as three.

The denial stage is the first normal response. We cannot believe what we are hearing, or seeing. We feel numb, that what is happening is like being in a dream. We walk about like a robot, doing what must be done. We tell ourselves this can't be real. Yet, we soon discover it is. Now what? Where do we turn? How do we cope?

· · ·

DISCUSSION:
1. Were you aware of the normal stages of grieving prior to your tragedy?
2. Did you know others who are grieving have feelings similar to yours?
3. How long did you feel numb, like you were walking about in a fog?
4. Did you think problems only happen to others and not to you.

· · ·

SCRIPTURE:
Psalm 142:3 "When my spirit grows faint within me, it is you who know my way. In the path where I walk men have hidden a snare for me."
Psalm 121:1-2 "I lift up my eyes to the hills—where does my help come from? My help comes from the LORD, the Maker of heaven and earth."
Psalm 102:2 "Do not hide your face from me, when I am in distress. Turn your ear to me; when I call, answer me quickly."

· · ·

PRAYER:
Lord, you take over when I am too numb to make decisions and direct me in the way I should go. Amen.

WHY DID THIS HAPPEN?

If I just knew why…!

When my daughter died, her pastor spoke from the 11th chapter of John at her funeral. As he discussed the story of Mary and Martha I saw parallels between these two women and my own life. Mary and Martha lived in Bethany with their brother Lazarus. All three were friends of Jesus and he visited with them often. When Lazarus got sick, Mary and Martha did everything they could do for him. I'm sure they spent much time in prayer. They also sent a message to Jesus saying, "The one you love is sick."

As it was when Lazarus became sick, so too, when Lonnie was burned, prayer went up all over the area to Jesus, saying, "the one you love is sick." Since Jesus was healing people and Lazarus was a good friend of his, Mary and Martha expected Jesus to come quickly to heal their brother. But, Jesus didn't come right away, rather he waited four days. Lazarus died and Jesus told his disciples, "The sickness will not end in death. No, it is for God's glory so that God's son may be glorified through it."

When Lonnie was so ill, I expected Jesus to heal her too, even if it took a long time. I told my Lord often, "I am a nurse and my friends are nurses. We will take care of Lonnie for as long as needed to help her return to health. We are trusting your healing hand for a complete recovery." God did not choose to heal her. My Lonnie died.

I asked God what glory He could bring out of her death? I still don't understand. I did, and still do ask, "Why, Lord?"

I haven't gotten the answer I long for, but I have received the comfort I need from Jesus.

Some folks say, "Don't ask why!" I don't have any qualms about asking why. Our Lord spent three years teaching a motley crew of men how to be Christians and evangelists, and they often asked why. He taught them, discussed things with them. He had great patience with them when they had questions. He has had great patience with me, too, as I look to him and say, "Why Lord, why my daughter?"

If you are asking why today, don't let anybody make you feel guilty about it. God loves you and me so much. He created us, he knows us well, and he understands our need to search for answers. Who better to ask than Him.

·   ·   ·

DISCUSSION: We have heard many times that God has reasons for what happens in life. We do not always like to hear that when we are facing a loss.

1. Can you remember a time with some problem that you asked. "Why Lord?" How did He answer?
2. Give an example of someone you know who survived and was able to use their own loss and pain to help others.
3. Should you feel guilty because you want to know why?
4. Does God really care about our problems and how we feel today?

·   ·   ·

SCRIPTURE:
II Cor. 1:3,4 "Praise be to the God and Father of our Lord Jesus Christ, the Father of compassion and the God of all comfort, who

comforts us in all our troubles, so that we can comfort those in any trouble with the comfort we ourselves have received from God."
Eph. 2:10 "For we are God's workmanship, created in Christ Jesus to do good works, which God prepared in advance for us to do."
Jer. 15:19b "If you utter worthy, not worthless words, you will be my spokesman."

• • •

PRAYER:
Lord help us know that someday when we stand in your presence You will answer our "why" questions in your own way. Amen.

ANGER

While in the anger stage of grieving, fury, rage and resentment are uppermost in the mind. After accepting the fact that the accident happened it is normal to then become angry and ask why it happened. During this stage of grieving many law suits are started. We are looking for someone or something to blame by thinking, "Someone is going to pay for all my pain."

I remember during my own anger stage standing in the middle of my kitchen yelling at God after my beautiful 26-year-old daughter died. I did not blame God for her death. After seeing the extent of her burns, and the overwhelming pain and infection in her body I looked to Him as a merciful God for taking her home.

But, when I yelled at God, it was: "Why did you let her strike that match? You could have stopped her before she struck it." I was angry. I was blaming God for letting the situation happen in the first place.

Both anger and blame are normal during this stage. We also get angry at friends, neighbors, relatives. We feel they do not visit often enough. They do not really care. They do not really understand how bad "I" feel. They can become the object of our anger if they have healthy family members—we become angry at them because one of ours has died.

We may even be angry at the person who died. We may feel that the person left us when we still needed them, even if it was an accident that the dead person did not cause. Take comfort in the fact that the anger will subside as we work through our grief. Pray and ask God to replace it with His wonderful peace.

· · ·

DISCUSSION: You can expect angry feelings to overwhelm you at times during your grieving. This is normal. It is important that you not let your anger smolder inside for long periods of time.

1. Who can you call when you need someone to talk to about your concerns?
2. Why is it important to get control of our anger before it continues inside for long periods of time?
3. What problems arise when you keep your hurts and concerns bottled up inside and do not talk about them?
4. Why is talking to others therapeutic?

· · ·

SCRIPTURE:

Psalm 37:8 "Refrain from anger and turn from wrath, do not fret—it leads only to evil."

Prov. 29:22 "An angry man stirs up dissension."

James 1:19,20 "My dear brothers, take note of this. Everyone should be quick to listen, slow to speak, and slow to become angry, for man's anger does not bring about the righteous life that God desires."

Eph. 4:26 "In your anger do not sin. Do not let the sun go down while you are still angry."

· · ·

PRAYER:

Lord help us not to stay angry. Help us be available to others and to listen when someone needs to talk. Calm the storm inside us and help us not be crippled by our loss. Amen.

CRYING

How many times in our youth did an adult tell us "Don't cry", when we suffer a minor fall or injury. Little boys often hear, "Big boys don't cry." Big Boys do cry, big men cry, as do little and big girls.

In our culture crying is discouraged. Friends expect us, even when grieving, to act as if nothing has happened when the most valued person in our life is no longer with us. Many times grievers will delay returning to grocery stores, church and other familiar places because they fear they will burst into tears. We as grievers wouldn't mind for ourselves, but those around us become uneasy when we cry in public.

Tears can be expected when:
1. We hear a song our loved one enjoyed.
2. We meet friends we enjoyed together.
3. We return to a restaurant, church or social club where we shared good experiences.
4. We smell the scent of loved one's cologne or perfume.
5. Someone asks the cause of death and we discuss the recent past.
6. Discussing memories with others.
7. Anything shared previously can trigger tears.

Tears early in our grief experience run easily whether we try to suppress them or not. As we work through our grief we can go longer periods without crying. In time, we can return to our normal routine with only minimal episodes of tears.

In our grief support group meetings we put boxes of tissues on the table so folks know as we talk this is an acceptable place to cry.

Avoid saying to a grieving person, "Get hold of yourself", "Control yourself", or similar statements in a stern manner. This makes people think they should not grieve or cry, when in reality crying is exactly what is needed. Experts in bereavement work agree that crying is normal. Crying is healthy. God gave us tear ducts to use when we are sad. There is healing in tears. Let them flow freely. Be available to hug, touch an arm or stand beside to help in any way. Be a good friend. Crying releases pressure that builds up inside us when we have a major loss and helps us heal.

• • •

DISCUSSION: It is OK to cry, men and women, boys and girls, any age can, and need, to cry over losses.
1. When did tears come unexpectedly? Discuss the circumstances.
2. How did people around you react?
3. Did you feel better after you cried?
4. Should you care how others respond to your grieving?
5. Why is crying important as you work through your grief?
6. What examples do you know in scripture that deal with crying?

• • •

SCRIPTURE:
1. **2 Samuel 1:12** David at the death of Saul and Jonathan
2. **2 Kings 13:14** Jehoash at the death of Elisha
3. **John 11:35** Jesus over his friend Lazarus

4. **Isaiah 25:8** "He will swallow up death forever. The Sovereign Lord will wipe away the tears from all faces."

·   ·   ·

PRAYER:

Help us Lord not to be ashamed, and to let the tears fall. As they do, bring healing to the hearts of your grieving people. Amen.

UNREALISTIC EXPECTATIONS

A reporter once asked people walking on the sidewalk in a large city, "How long does it take to get over the death of a family member?" The responses ranged from 48 hours to two weeks. The people approached had obviously never grieved.

As Christians, we do the same things to ourselves. We feel that because we are believers, we should not be feeling the anger or depression that is normal to grieving. We think we should be able to cope better.

Grief is an open wound. It is more traumatic than major surgery or a fracture. It takes much longer to heal. Because we are believers, we expect immediate healing. Although Jesus could do that, He often chooses to let us go through the normal grieving phases. There are no shortcuts. Step by step, little by little, the steps become less painful, and the days easier to endure.

The usual length of time for our grieving is about two years, depending on circumstances and support systems.

Grievers may heal in less than two years if they have a loving, close knit family that encourages, visits and phones often. When living physically close, daily concerns can be voiced to each other. Support group members or church family can provide this same service. A friend can invite and/or escort a griever to church functions, including him or her in activities that do not expend a lot of energy or concentration. Those in the process of healing lack both. If they try something simple and fail, it is depressing to the griever. It's a reminder that they are not functioning as they were before their loved one's death. If they try something simple and succeed, the accomplishment can be praised and is a positive step in their healing.

We shouldn't expect that when we become Christians that we give up our humanness. We feel the same feelings as unbelievers while we learn to cope with an empty house, an empty spot at the table, the loss of a confidant and best friend. Our routine for our life changes drastically. We make new routines—this time alone.

.   .   .

DISCUSSION: Before we grievers are met with a tragic situation we do not know about the normal process of grieving.

1. Were you surprised that you were not totally recovered in a short period of time?
2. Did you think because you are a Christian you wouldn't feel as much pain as a non-Christian?
3. Did you think you were losing your mind as you dealt with a mix of feelings?
4. Were you aware that this is a part of normal grieving?
5. What other unrealistic ideas or thinking have you faced?

.   .   .

SCRIPTURE:

I Peter 4:12 "Dear friends, do not be surprised at the painful trial you are suffering, as though something strange were happening to you."

II Cor 12:8,9 "Three times I pleaded with the Lord to take it away from me. But He said to me, "My grace is sufficient for you, for my power is made perfect in weakness. Therefore I will boast all the more gladly about my weaknesses, so that Christ's power may rest on me."

· · ·

PRAYER:
Lord help us to know that you never promised to spare us from the hurts of life, but you did promise to be with us through all our problems. Thank you for that. Amen.

THE GUILTS

When a loved one dies, most of us can probably think of something that was left undone. Our guilt feelings may be real or imagined. We may wish we would have said, "I love you", more often or baked their favorite cake instead of putting it off until another day.

When I think back on my life with my daughter, I wish I had spent more time with her, just enjoying her company. Now I can think of many times when I let something get in the way of our relationship, times I wish I could change. The memories are painful because it is too late now.

Guilt may come in the form of reliving in our minds the way our loved one died. We may try to think of a way we could have prevented it from happening:

1. Could a doctor have been called sooner?
2. Did I miss a sign or a symptom of impending problems that I should have seen?
3. Was I always available when my presence was needed or desired?
4. Am I a good person or did I fail my loved one when he or she needed me the most?
5. Can I ever forgive myself for whatever it is I may have done and didn't?

We may need to ask ourselves if the regrets we have in our minds, that cause us to feel guilty, are really important. We tend to dwell on small things, blaming ourselves to excess, heaping more distress on our already hurting selves.

We are all human. Any day we can see things we could have done and omitted, or should not have done, and did. After a death, we tend to magnify these negatives, blowing them out of proportion.

It is comforting to know that these are normal, natural questions we have following a death. We may search and seek answers, but let us not allow our guilt feelings to consume us. We need to forgive ourselves and others for whatever the circumstances that surround our loved one's death.

• • •

DISCUSSION: My loved one has died. Now these questions plague me.

1. What did I do that I should not have done?
2. What did I not do, that I should have?
3. If I had done something more would it really have made a life or death change in circumstances?
4. Are my guilt feelings over something truly important?
5. Can God forgive me? Can I forgive myself?

• • •

SCRIPTURE:

I John 1:9 "If we confess our sins, he is faithful and just and will forgive us our sins and purify us from all unrighteousness."

Psalm 38:4 "My guilt has overwhelmed me like a burden too heavy to bear."

Psalm 38:21 "0 Lord, do not forsake me, be not far from me, O my God."

· · ·

PRAYER:

Help us Lord not to allow our guilt feelings to paralyze us. Help us to know that we are forgiven by our loving, living Lord. Help us to forgive ourselves of any real, or imagined, infractions. Help us be grateful You are beside us no matter what problem or concern we are facing today. Amen.

DEPRESSION

When I realized my daughter would never again run into my house with an enthusiastic, "Hi Mom", I became very depressed. The emotion of depression is normal. You may feel that any goals or expectations you had for the future are gone. Your direction is changed.

I, myself, will never again depend on my daughter for an opinion or a decision. I will never have her assistance for a project in the days ahead.

The remembrances of her time with me were frequently in my thoughts. Although this could be positive, because she was no longer physically with me, I needed to find someone else to fill the vacant spots in my life. Maybe you have that problem too. You may be wandering to get out of this depression that is a constant companion.

My friend Lynn said, after her husband was killed, "I sat for three months and looked out a window. I could not do anything. I didn't care about my appearance or what happened around me. I didn't care if I combed my hair, washed my face or ate. Nothing mattered."

This is how you may feel after someone you love dies. It takes a long time and a lot of family support to progress through this very difficult stage of grieving.

You think you will never laugh again, but someday you will.

The best way to stop being down is to look up from the difficulty to the God who heals. Listen to Christian radio. Music can be helpful, the words of the songs reassure that God loves you and sees your pain. He answers prayer. He walks with you through the valleys and shadows. He never leaves you. Whether you feel His closeness or not He is there.

• • •

DISCUSSION: Depression is like a black cloud that settles over us, causing us to close ourselves from the rest of the world.
1. What things did you have most difficulty accomplishing during your "down" times?
2. What, or who, helped you to get out of your depressed state?
3. Do you still have days when depression returns?
4. What suggestions do you have for others so that they can help themselves?
5. How can you help a specific person during their depression?
6. Discuss depression with family doctor.

• • •

SCRIPTURE:
Psalm 42:5 "Why are you downcast, Oh My soul? Why so disturbed within me? Put your hope in God…"
Psalm 142:4, "Look to my right and see, no one is concerned for me, I have no refuge, no one cares for my life. I cry to you, O Lord…"
Psalm 37:39 "The salvation of the righteous comes from the Lord, He is their stronghold in time of trouble…"

• • •

PRAYER:
Lord we do not feel your closeness today. Lift us up, we cannot do it ourselves. Lead us as we walk through our grief that we might smile again. You are our salvation. Amen.

THE LONELINESS

My friend Lucille expressed her loneliness to me when she said, "The most difficult thing for me to do is walk into that empty house." Loneliness is a common problem for widows and widowers. You can keep yourself busy going places and doing things all the day long, but the time comes when you must return home to the empty house, the empty bed.

Some folks have said they keep a radio or television on at all times just to hear the sound of another voice in the house which is helpful to them. You may want to change the furniture around so you do not look at an empty place at the table where your loved one sat or his special chair where he watched TV. You may choose to rent out a room in your home to some young person for company or have a friend or family member move in for a while. You may choose to just work at your new life alone working out your own special ways to cope with your loneliness.

Whatever way you feel is best for you, try new things to cope with this feeling of loss. Try to accept that it is normal to feel this way after a loss. Keep trying to do things so that you won't feel as lonely.

Try to read or do crafts for short periods of time. Volunteer at community projects, such as hospital gift shops, library programs, etc. These programs are helpful to others and you will find you are helping yourself as well. What were your interests and talents prior to your loss? Consider returning to one activity on a part-time basis at first, increasing your involvement as you feel able to do so. Be as busy as you want to be without overextending your energy. As you heal, you will also need rest time.

. . .

DISCUSSION: Making a new life alone is a most difficult part of grief work.

1. What are some of the "alone" things that you face since the death of your loved one?
2. How are you coping with each of the above?
3. What have others done to help you?
4. What could others have done to help you?
5. How will these experiences help you to help someone else?

. . .

SCRIPTURE:
> **Psalm 31:12** "I am forgotten by them as though I were dead, I have become like broken pottery."
> **Psalm 68:5, 6** "A father to the fatherless, a defender of widows is God in His holy dwelling. God sets the lonely in families."
> **Psalm 91:1** "He who dwells in the shelter of the Most High will rest in the shadow of the Almighty."

. . .

PRAYER:
Lord you are always near to care for us. Help us to be as families to those among us who feel that no one cares. When the family is not there, let the church family and individuals draw close to each other and be families.

Help us see the need in others even though they smile when we meet. Make us aware of the real problems others are facing. Help us not to dwell only on our own troubles, but to reach out to those around us, in love. Amen.

PHYSICAL AND EMOTIONAL SYMPTOMS

Some of the symptoms most commonly seen in grieving persons are the following:

1. Crying
2. Sleeplessness
3. Either no appetite, or overeating
4. Remembering the loved one in loving ways (even if they had caused terrible hurt to you at times)
5. Hating the person for leaving you (they knew I still needed them)
6. Guilt feelings
7. A temporary wish to join the loved one in death
8. Blaming circumstances
9. Blaming a person, hospital, doctor, or staff
10. Fear of losing control in public
11. Inability to function even with personal care
12. Yearning for the person that died
13. Anger at God for allowing it
14. Apprehension when going back to significant places following death
15. Depression symptoms include the following:

1. Dry mouth
2. Inability to concentrate
3. Frequent sighing
4. Constant exhaustion
5. Empty feeling
6. Numbness
7. Sad expression on face
8. Pacing or sitting and staring

Do not worry. Your physical health will return and you will work through the varied emotions. You will again be motivated to return to society. Until you can, seek support and encouragement through those who have been there. People can help you, whether they be family, friends, church family or professional care givers. You may not see it yet, but there is light at the end of the tunnel.

• • •

DISCUSSION: Sometimes folks think they are losing their minds or that a disease has attacked their physical bodies, when in reality they are suffering from normal grief symptoms.
1. What symptoms do you find most difficult to overcome?
2. Were you aware that the terrible way you were feeling was part of your grieving?
3. Does it help to learn that grief causes many reactions in people that are misunderstood by others?
4. How can you help others to be aware of normal grieving?

• • •

SCRIPTURE:
Psalm 147:3 "He heals the brokenhearted and binds up their wounds."

Psalm 34:18 "The Lord is close to the brokenhearted and saves those who are crushed in spirit."

Psalm 34:19 "A righteous man may have many troubles but the Lord delivers him from them all."

•　　•　　•

PRAYER:

Lord help us to be sensitive to the normal reactions we have to our grief in ourselves and in others. Help us turn to you and find the peace that fills our broken hearts. Amen.

ONLY MAKE LITTLE DECISIONS

Sometimes we are tempted after one we love has died, to make big decisions that will affect the rest of our lives. I was told of one woman who, following the death of her husband, quickly sold her home, everything she owned and moved to Florida to start a new life. She soon became aware that she had not only lost her mate, but that now she had also lost the support system that could have helped her: her family, friends, church family and neighbors.

She thought she should be able to start over, but the unresolved grief followed her. It still needed to be faced and now she was trying to do it alone. The familiar house and friends are a form of security to us.

Big decisions can wait until we have worked through our grief. It will be wiser when we are able to give adequate and clear thinking to our situation before making major changes.

• • •

DISCUSSION: Everyday we are faced with decisions some larger, some smaller.
1. What decisions did you find the most difficult to make?
2. How long did it take you to make a decision?

3. Was it easier if someone visited with whom you could discuss your problem?
4. Do the littlest decisions now, seem as big as the largest decisions of the past?

• • •

SCRIPTURE:

James 1:5 "If any of you lack wisdom, let him ask of God, who gives generously to all without finding fault, and it will be given to him."

Psalm 37:7 "Be still before the Lord and wait patiently for him."

Prov. 20:18 "Make plans by seeking advice."

• • •

PRAYER:

Lord, even though we are grieving, help us to be aware that you are the answer to all of our problems. Help us make wise decisions and know that you are always available to help your people. Amen.

YOUR PHYSICAL HEALTH

When you have lost someone you love, you may just want to lie in bed or sit in a favorite chair, unable to motivate yourselves to any of your normal activity. At this time, you need to be aware that grieving takes a huge amount of energy and is a high stress experience. Your physical bodies are affected.

You may lose some weight due to your lack of appetite or your desire to fix food for yourself. Eating small amounts of something nutritious like fresh fruit or ice cream during the day is one way to guarantee that you get some nourishment. Sometimes a big meal is just too much to handle, even if someone else prepares it. Eating frequent small amounts may help you swallow.

You may need to visit your family physician. Be aware that if you have another health problem that needs monitoring, such as diabetes, heart problems or blood pressure problems, this can worsen with the additional stress of irregular eating and sleeping patterns that develop as you grieve.

You need to remember to continue medications as previously ordered for these conditions, and to take them as they are prescribed. It is important not to skip doses or forget to take them altogether.

Walking is one of the best ways to decrease the stress level. You can start with a short walk in the fresh air. You may have to make up your mind that you are going to do this whether you feel like it or not. It may help you to be motivated if you are encouraging others to do the same.

After you are walking a few minutes and short distances, you can increase your goals until you are walking a half-hour or an hour. You may start with a five-minute walk increasing it the next week to ten minutes, etc.

Look around as you walk. Try to enjoy God's world, and tell Him so. You may find that you can talk to God best as you walk.

• • •

DISCUSSION: It is difficult to get back to normal routines after a loss.
1. In what ways are you aware that you have neglected yourself?
2. What can you make yourself do to change this?
3. Does calling a supportive friend and asking him or her to do something with you help rather than doing it alone?
4. Are diet, fresh air, and exercise really important?

• • •

SCRIPTURE:
Psalm 31:9 "Be merciful to me, O Lord, for I am in distress, my eyes grow weak with sorrow, my soul and my body with grief."
Psalm 38:6 "I am bowed down and brought very low, all day long I go about mourning. My back is filled with searing pain, there is no health in my body. I am feeble and utterly crushed, I groan in anguish of heart."
Psalm 38:22 "Come quickly to help me, O Lord my Savoir."

• • •

PRAYER:

Help us to take good care of the physical body you have given us so that we have the energy to deal with the grief work ahead. Lead us to total healing as only you, the Healer, can do. Amen.

INTENSITY AND DURATION

The grief process is harder and lasts longer with some than others, depending on several things:

1. The relationship to the deceased—For example, if the loss is a parent or neighbor, the grief will be more painful than if the deceased is a relative who had lived in another state for the past 20 years.
2. Your childhood or adult experiences—If this is your first experience with death, it will hit you harder than those who have lost loved ones close together.
3. If the person that died was someone who was depended upon for financial, physical or emotional support, it will be very hard.
4. Age and level of maturity.
5. The nature of the dying process—Was the death sudden and violent, or a prolonged illness where death was expected?
6. The condition of the body—whether it was viewable or not.
7. The body—if missing in action, or buried at sea. You need to see the body or you always have a slight doubt in your mind that your loved one may really not have died.
8. Circumstances of the death—Was it the result of someone

else's carelessness or neglect, an unnecessary death, or an inevitable death?

9. Religious beliefs. If you feel that you will see your loved one again in heaven, you have an eternal hope that helps you deal with the loss.

10. Support of family and friends—Those people who have good support systems progress through grieving more easily than those who have no one to help them work their way through the painful days.

• • •

DISCUSSION: Death snatches away our loved ones in various ways.
1. How did the circumstances surrounding the death of your loved one effect your grieving?
2. What past experiences have you had with death?
3. How did past experiences effect your current grieving?
4. Did past experiences make grieving longer or shorter, more painful or less painful?
5. How does your age or maturity relate to your grief?

• • •

SCRIPTURE:
I Peter 5:6, 7 "Humble yourselves, therefore, under God's mighty hand, that he may lift you up in due time. Cast all your anxiety on him because he cares for you."
I Peter 5:10 "And the God of all grace, who called you to his eternal glory in Christ, after you have suffered a little while, will Himself restore you and make you strong, firm and steadfast."

• • •

PRAYER:

Lord, we wonder how long will this pain and sorrow continue to overwhelm us? Help us to be aware of your presence. Help us lean on you as our source of strength. Make us aware that you never leave us or forsake us, even when our grief stretches out longer than we would choose. Thank you, Lord, that you are faithful. Amen.

DRUGS AND ALCOHOL

Often, well-meaning friends will encourage you to take a little pill or a little drink to help you cope with your problems during grieving. You are at a vulnerable point in your life and you tend to grab at anything anyone suggests that will ease the pain or help you rest when the sleepless nights stretch out before you one after another.

A word of caution. A little drink or a little pill may help temporarily, but the problems are still to be faced when the pill and drink wear off. Some people find themselves increasing the pills and increasing the drinks until the original problem of facing their grief is compounded, and they face a growing dependence on drugs and/or alcohol, or both.

Grief, is enough to face. By covering up the symptoms by self-induced numbness, you prolong the original problem and your healing is extended.

•　　•　　•

DISCUSSION: Numbing ourselves from the pain of our loss is something we all desire, however we need to be very careful when certain methods come our way.

1. Does taking drugs or alcohol after a loss help?

2. Is the original problem still there when the effects of the drugs and/or alcohol wear off?
3. How long should "temporary" aids be used or should they at all?
4. Is it really important that I face this pain?
5. Will the pain ever go away?

• • •

SCRIPTURE:
Eph. 5:15 "Be very careful, then, how you live, not as unwise but as wise."
Eph. 5:18 "Do not get drunk on wine, which leads to debauchery. Instead, be filled with the Spirit."
Eph. 6:10 "Finally, be strong in the Lord and in his mighty power."
Philippians 4:13 "I can do everything through him who gives me strength."

• • •

PRAYER:
Lord, help us lean on You rather than a chemical crutch to get us through difficult days. Thank you that You are able to keep us from falling. Amen.

MAKING BARGAINS WITH GOD

You may go through times when you will try to make bargains with God, over your losses. You say, "I will do anything. I will start going to church, treat my family better, stay home more, read the Bible, stop smoking…" You say what you think will impress God, if only this problem will cease. You hope it will only be a bad dream, a nightmare, that you will wake up soon to life the way it was.

You may pray, "God, do not let my loved one be dead or dying. The pain inside me is too much to bear. Take it away. Don't let it be true. I cannot handle this horrible problem."

Tragedies do lead us closer to God in some instances. You pray, you read your Bible, seeking some way to change your circumstances. You seek to change God's mind about what is happening.

If you, yourselves, are aware you are dying you may also try to bargain with God— First, for a cure or total healing. If this doesn't happen, you may bargain for time, saying, "OK God, I am going to die, but please do not let it happen until my house is paid for or my child finishes college or a grandchild is born." What ever is important at this time in your life are the things you'll try to bargain for.

Bargaining is normal. No one wants to face tragedies including death and would rather avoid them or put them off until a more opportune time. Our choice would be good health and a long, happy life; thus we bargain when this evades us.

• • •

DISCUSSION: As we go over the tragedy we are facing, it is natural to allow ourselves extra time to think clearly. This time helps us to face the problem and the days ahead.

1. What kind of bargains have you found yourself making with God?
2. Did this help you as you worked through your grief?
3. Were you aware that bargaining is normal?
4. Do you have trouble accepting His decisions when it comes to yourself and those you love?

• • •

SCRIPTURE:

2 Sam. 12:22, 23 He (David) answered, "While the child was still alive, I fasted and wept, I thought, Who knows? The Lord may be gracious to me and let the child live. But now that he is dead, why should I fast? Can I bring him back again? I will go to him, but he will not return to me."

Psalm 32:8 "I will instruct you and teach you in the way you should go, I will counsel you and watch over you."

• • •

PRAYER:

Lord, this nightmare we face is too much for us. Thank you for standing beside us as we deal with our loss. Thank you for understanding our bargains during tragic times that started during Old Testament days and continues today. Amen.

LISTENING AS THERAPY

The best way to support someone who is grieving is to be a good listener. A griever does not need, or want, advice. They need to talk.

You may find yourself hearing the same stories over and over day after day. Grieving people may not remember what they told you. They may stop part way through a story and say, "Oh, I remember now I did tell you that."

The need to talk about the person that died is very important. People who are grieving need to relive the good times verbally. You will find they play down the bad times and elevate the good conversations and experiences. Keep in mind that this is normal.

When a grieving person comes to you for support remember to be available, be a good listener, touch, hug and show outward signs that you care.

• • •

DISCUSSION: Knowing when to listen is as important as knowing when to talk.

1. Do you have a special person in mind who you know is a good listener?

2. Were you aware, before your loss, of the importance of listening?

3. Have you seen the healing and peace that comes as you repeat, in detail, the story of your pain to another person?
4. Have you committed to being a good listener to your friends in the days ahead?

·   ·   ·

SCRIPTURE:

James 3:18 "Peacemakers who sow in peace, raise a harvest of righteousness."

James 1:19 "My dear brothers, take note of this. Everyone should be quick to listen, slow to speak and slow to become angry."

Prov. 23:19 "Listen my son and be wise, and keep your heart on the right path."

·   ·   ·

PRAYER:

Thank you, Lord, for listening as we pour out our hearts to you. Help us to listen to others in the same loving way. Amen.

WORDS THAT HURT

After a loved one dies, it is common to remember words that rubbed like sandpaper in our open wound. If a person has never grieved, he may find himself saying the wrong thing as he approaches the grieving person at a viewing, funerals or soon after the death. It is natural to want to express words of comfort, but many people don't know what to say. Some people refuse to go to viewing and funerals for this reason.

Lets look at some words that can be hurtful:

1. "Do not cry—get hold of yourself." crying is normal
2. "Men do not cry—control yourself." men do cry, they need to cry
3. "I know how you feel." It's sometimes better not to say this if you've never grieved for a loved one
4. "Time heals." Maybe so, but I am in pain now
5. "God wanted another angel in heaven." Then let him create another one, not take someone I love away from me
6. "He or she is better off, they suffered so much." Well, I am not better off. I am suffering now, can you see that?
7. "You are lucky to have your children." Yes, but they can never replace the one person that died. If they are young, the responsibility of raising them alone is overwhelming

8. If it is a baby:— "You are young, you can have other children." You act like this one didn't matter, I may have others, but I loved this one too.

9. "God has his reasons for this." That does not take away the pain I feel at this moment.

10. "You are lucky you have a job." I am not even sure I can make it through today. How can I think about returning to work.

11. "Everybody has problems, you are not the only one. You will get over it."

Let us be careful as we talk to others. It may help if you put yourself in the griever's place. Consider if what you are about to say will help or hurt. Your friend is already in pain, and you don't want to add to it. Often just being there is the most important thing you can do for a grieving person.

• • •

DISCUSSION: Since we have listed words that hurt, consider the fact that this may be a time when words are not the thing needed most.

1. What can you do that grieving people will remember?

2. What has been done for you that was most helpful, or most hurtful, when you were going through your grieving period?

3. Are you aware of how important touching and hugging are to the griever. These are signs that you care.

4. Do you agree that one important thing you can do is to visit and be available?

• • •

SCRIPTURE:

Prov. 15:1 "A gentle answer turns away wrath, but a harsh word stirs up anger."

Matt. 24:35 "Heaven and earth will pass away, but my words will never pass away."

Prov. 16:23, 24 "A wise man's heart guides his mouth, and his lips promote instruction. Pleasant words are a honeycomb, sweet to the soul and healing to the bones."

•　•　•

PRAYER:

Help us, Lord, to be aware of the words we use as we try to help others. Thank you that we can depend on Your word of comfort that comes from Your Word, the Bible. Amen.

WAYS TO HELP

It is hard, at times, to know what to say to a grieving person. Sometimes saying nothing is best. One thing is sure—no matter what is said or done, the pain of initial grieving is not going to go away immediately.

You can ask if there is anything you can do to help the grieving person. Many times the griever is in such a shocked state that she or he is not aware of what needs to be done. You may need to assess the situation yourself, and help in what ever way you can. You may answer the phone and write down messages for the griever to look at later. You may wash the dishes or care for children. You may just sit beside the griever and be available. You may just listen as she talks about her loved one, hug her, let her cry.

The grieving person may want you to go along as he/she picks out a casket, views the body or does any of the tasks that must be done immediately following a death. The most important thing to keep in mind is that just being available for whatever is needed is sometimes the most helpful.

• • •

DISCUSSION: As we approach a grieving family, we often do not know what to do to help.

1. What did someone do that helped you the most?
2. Was the person you expected to be the most supportive the one who helped you the most, or did someone else fill that role?
3. After grieving does the experience enable you to call or visit future grievers and be more helpful to them?
4. Who should be helping—family, church family, friends or professionals?

•　•　•

SCRIPTURE:
    Prov. 15:4 "The tongue that brings healing is a tree of life."
    1 Tim. 5:3 "Give proper recognition to those widows who are really in need."
    1 John 4:11 "Dear friends, since God so loved us, we also ought to love one another."
    James 2:26 "As the body without the spirit is dead, so faith without deeds is dead."

•　•　•

PRAYER:
Lord, open our eyes to the needs around us and help us to be available to others in pain. We are now more aware of how important the support of another can be as we struggle through difficult days ourselves. Help us remember how you have helped us, as we help others. Amen.

ANTICIPATORY AND PREPARATORY GRIEVING

When we have been told that someone we love is dying, it is natural to begin grieving before they die, without being aware that the process is happening. This is called anticipatory, or preparatory, grieving because we are preparing ourselves for a change. We are anticipating how we will handle our life without our loved one.

If our husband is dying we may wonder how we will manage without the financial support. We may need to return to the work-a-day world for the money we need to pay our bills. We may think about how we can care for a home alone, or children alone. We may think, "What do I do when I have a flat tire, the furnace stops working, or the lawn mower will not start?"

This anticipatory period of time helps us collect our thoughts and organize coping methods that help to deal with the impending death. This is also the time when we need to check the insurance policy, see that the will is in order and details of the funeral considered.

Preparatory grieving has helped a lot of people because it allows them to work through a gamut of emotions prior to the expected death. That does not mean there will be no grieving after the death. There will be. However, it may not last as long or be as intense because of the grief work already done.

· · ·

DISCUSSION: The days are long, the road tedious as we stand beside a loved one who will soon close eyes in death.

1. In what ways did others help the most?
2. Were you surprised at the mix of emotions you felt when death did come, because you thought you had yourself well prepared to face the end?
3. In what ways did your prior preparation for the event make it easier on you and your family?
4. Do you have fewer regrets since you had time to say goodbye?

· · ·

SCRIPTURE:

2 Cor. 4:16, 18 "Therefore we do not lose heart. Though outwardly we are wasting away, yet inwardly we are being renewed day by day. So we fix our eyes not on what is seen, but on what is unseen. For what is seen is temporary, but what is unseen is eternal."

Psalm 23:4 "Even though I walk through the valley of the shadow of death, I will fear no evil, for You are with me."

Psalm 116:15 "Precious in the sight of the Lord is the death of his saints."

· · ·

PRAYER:

Hold us up, Lord, as we face our own death or the death of the ones we love. Help us to always know we are never alone, You are always with us. Amen.

THOSE SPECIAL DAYS

You will hear grieving people say, "The hardest day for me is _____", and they will relate some special event that is a direct reminder of the good days before the one they loved died. One of the biggest is Christmas, when family members get together and enjoy meals, gift giving, trimming the tree or other special traditions.

Other holidays that often spark special memories are Thanksgiving, birthdays, wedding anniversaries, Valentines Day, Easter, family reunions and picnics.

One of the hardest for me is Mother's Day, when my daughter always stood for a long time reading cards before she found one that said exactly what she wanted.

I had been with her many times when she searched out those special cards for someone else, thus, I can picture her doing it for me at Mother's Day times. She would also tell me that it took a long time to find just the right card, which of course makes it more meaningful.

As a special day approaches, ask a friend or family member to schedule some activity that will keep the mind and body occupied on that day. Don't let yourself be home alone wallowing in self-pity as you remember the good times past and remind yourself of the loss of the present. The loss is always there but a busy day will keep you from dwelling on it and make it less difficult to endure. The first special day is the hardest—Christmas, anniversary, birthday, etc. Each successive special day will be less intense.

. . .

DISCUSSION: Special days are connected to special memories.
1. What can I do to help someone who is hurting to more easily get through those special days?
2. Does anyone care, even Jesus?
3. What good memories of special days in the past can we discuss?
4. What could we do today to make new memories?
5. What new ministries could be started for special people on special days?

. . .

SCRIPTURE:
Matthew 7:12 "So in everything, do to others what you would have them do to you."
Isaiah 61:1b "He has sent me to bind up the broken hearted."
I Peter 5:7 "Cast all your anxiety on him because he cares for you."
Psalm 46:1 "God is our refuge and strength, an ever-present help in trouble."

. . .

PRAYER:
Lord, help us get through the "special days." Help us have good memories, and look to them to bring joy to our hearts today. Amen.

OTHER MAJOR LOSSES

Whenever we have a major loss, we will go through stages of grief until we work our way through to acceptance. Some of the major losses we may encounter are listed below:

1. Divorce
2. A severe mentally, or physically, impaired child is born
3. A fire that takes away everything we own
4. The loss of an arm, leg or breast to disease or injury
5. A business that fails
6. A runaway child
7. A stillborn baby
8. A miscarriage
9. A family moving to an unfamiliar area, especially against their will, such as members of armed forces families.

I am sure you can add other events to the above list that would be traumatic and cause the same thoughts, feelings, and emotions we deal with, as we are grieving our losses due to death. Let us not forget these people need our support also.

•   •   •

DISCUSSION: Some people think God deliberately hurts us for some reason. Let us remember that terrible things happen to all people just because we are human and live in a world of humans.

1. Can you remember a time when God helped you through a bad time, in a beautiful way?
2. How can a variety of losses be the same? How can they be different?
3. Since all major losses cause some grieving, should we be just as faithful in our support of others, regardless of the type of loss or pain they are currently enduring?
4. Ask yourself; "What can I do to help?" as others face trying times.

•   •   •

SCRIPTURE:

Lamentations 3:31-33 "For men are not cast off by the Lord forever. Though He brings grief, he will show compassion, so great is his unfailing love. For he does not willingly bring affliction or grief to the children of men."

Matt. 5:45b "He causes his sun to rise on the evil and the good, and sends rain on the righteous and the unrighteous."

Psalm 30:5b "Weeping may remain for a night but rejoicing comes in the morning."

•   •   •

PRAYER:

Let us see You, Lord, helping us pick up the pieces of our broken life and start over again after our loss. Thank you that as we go through the hard times in life, You are always there. Amen.

THE CHOICE IS YOURS

This is what the Lord says: "Put your house in order, because you are going to die; you will not recover." 2 Kings 20:1

We are a death-denying society. We make preparations for many other events in life, but we delay making preparations for the one thing that will happen to me and to you. Let me encourage you to do several things today:

1. Make a will or update your old one.
2. Check insurance policies, and increase coverage, if needed.
3. Decide which mortician, burial plots, etc, you would prefer.
4. Make family members aware of your desires and where important papers are being kept.
5. Have a serious talk with Jesus.

Review these verses and prayerfully ask Him if your personal relationships are in order.

The Roman Road:

Romans 3:25 - "For all have sinned and fall short of the glory of God."

Romans 3:10 - "There is no one righteous, not even one?"

Romans 6:23 - "For the wages of sin is death, but the gift of God is eternal life in Christ Jesus our Lord."

Romans 5:8, 9 - "But God demonstrates his own love for us in this: While we were still sinners, Christ died for us. Since we have now been justified by his blood, how much more shall we be saved from God's wrath through him."

Romans 10: 9, 10 - "That if you confess with your mouth Jesus is Lord, and believe in your heart that God raised him from the dead, you will be saved, For it is with your heart that you believe and are justified, and it is with your mouth that you confess and are saved."

Romans 10:13 - "Everyone who calls on the name of the Lord will be saved."

Why is the body in a casket so cold? Because the warm part of us, the living part of us, has gone to live somewhere else. Choose today where you want to live for eternity. The Lord wants you with Him in heaven, but the choice is yours.

John 11:25 Jesus said to her: "I am the resurrection and the life. He who believes in me will live, even though he dies, and whoever lives and believes in me will never die."

Do you believe this?

If you want to spend eternity in heaven with our Lord, pray something like this: Dear God, I am sorry for all the sins I have committed. Please forgive me. I want to be a part of the family of God. I ask you to come into my life and make me all that you created me to be, and let me live with you forever in heaven. In Jesus' Name. Amen.

To experience peace and begin a growth and healing process consider the following:

— Begin to read the Bible on a daily basis.
— Talk to Jesus in prayer on a daily basis.
— Find a Bible believing church and listen to the teaching of Gods' Word.

If this is what you choose, welcome to the family of God.

Scripture used in this book comes from:
The Ryrie Study Bible New International Version
Moody Press 1986

Psalm 31:12
Psalm 68:5,6
Psalm 91:1
I Peter 4:12
II Cor. 12:8,9
Psalm 37:8
Prov. 29:22
James 1:19,20
Eph. 2:10
Psalm 142:4
I John 1:9
Matt. 7:12
Psalm 46:1
II Kings 13:14
Psalm 147:3
Eph. 5:18
I Peter 5:6,7
Matt. 24:35
James 3:18
James 1:19
Prov. 23:19
James 1:5
Psalm 37:7
Prov. 20:18
Psalm 38:22
Eph. 4:26
Jer. 15:19b
Psalm 37:39
Psalm 38:4

Isa. 61:1b

Psalm 38:22

John 11:35

Psalm 34:18,19

Eph. 6:10

I Peter 5:10

Prov. 16:23,24

Prov. 15:4

I Tim. 5:3

I John 4:11

James 2:26

Psalm 23:4

Psalm 116:15

II Kings 20:1

II Cor. 1:3,4

Psalm 42:5

Psalm 32:8

Psalm 38:21

I Peter 5:7

II Sam 1:12

Isa, 25:8

Eph. 5:15

Phil. 4:13

Prov. 15:1

Lam. 3:31-33

Matt. 5:45b

Romans 3:10

Romans 10:9, 10

Psalm 121:1-2

Psalm 30:5b

Romans 6:23

Romans 10:13

Psalm 142:3

Romans 3:25
Romans 5:8,9
John 11:25
Psalm 102:2

Currently, Joan is a retired Registered Nurse, certified in psychiatric and mental health nursing. She, also, received National, Professional Certification as a Bereavement Facilitator from the American Academy of Bereavement, Tuscon, Arizona. 1994-2002

THE SURVIVORS: RECOVERY THROUGH GRIEF SUPPORT GROUPS was written by Joan Harmon. Available at local stores.

MORE OF THE SAME

If when you heal, you feel glad that you are healing well and never want to go through anything like a death of a loved one again. You could be right, but most of us as our life progresses will face this tragedy again.

In my past 20 years I have seen my parents face health problems and cared for them as they grew older and weaker. My father had aneurysms in his blood vessels. He died suddenly when one bleeding vessels broke in 1988. My mother had Alzheimer's. She died in 2002. My youngest son Michael joined the Navy after high school. He went through training and was assigned to a nuclear submarine, traveling a lot to foreign places. He left after 6 years and got a job at the Omaha, Nebraska Nuclear Power Plant.

One night he got severe abdominal pain and went to the emergency room. They could not find anything wrong by exams and xrays, sent him home saying it could be constipation. He went home sat down in his kitchen at the computer. That was at 12 midnight. He died at 1 AM. At autopsy the coroner found an open area in his bowel where it could not be seen by xray so surgery could be done. He died in 2005. Am I done with my grief? Only God knows and He is faithful and walks with us through every hurt when we turn to Him. So what should we do?

- Find a Bible believing Church
- Read His word
- Pray often
- Praise Him for loving us
- Love Him back
- Draw closer to Him